© Patricia Zeggelaar, 2020.

All rights reserved. No part of this publication may be reproduced, distributed, or transmitted in any form or by any means, including photocopying, recording, or other electronic or mechanical methods, without the prior written permission of the publisher, except in the case of brief quotations embodied in critical reviews and certain other noncommercial uses permitted by copyright law. For permission requests, write to the publisher: info@patriciaz.ca.

Back cover photograph taken by Bob Tabbiner Photography.

SPEAKING TRUTH TO FEAR

Practicing Hope in Difficult and
Challenging Times

Patricia Zeggelaar

INTRODUCTION

Fear. There is nothing this little 'f' word cannot destroy. I have witnessed, through my own experiences as well as those of my clients, how when we allow fear to drive our thoughts, feelings, and actions, we diminish our brilliance in the world. There is nothing fear cannot contaminate – our decision making, problem solving, and communication. It compromises our goals and dreams and damages our relationships, often severely and irrevocably.

I have worked on the front lines of conflict (fear's kissing cousin) within the corporate world for over 25 years. As a consultant and coach I have supported people at all levels within organizations understand the reality regarding fear's stronghold grip and influence.

Through my experiences I have learned fear is a cunning and convincing force and far more powerful than what most of us would like to acknowledge. I have come to think of fear as a thing – a beast – with a will of its own containing a singular and powerful message – 'No, don't'. This translates into our lives as 'No, don't have the conversation', 'No, don't take the risk', and 'No, don't rock the boat'. The ensuing carnage of allowing fear to have its way with us results in life and work experiences that feel diminished. We align our lives with an undue sense of worry and anxiety creating lack in meaning and happiness. We end up experiencing unnecessary pain and suffering all because of fear.

It doesn't have to be this way. Each of us has the ability to neutralize fear. Not by denying, avoiding, or ignoring it, because it turns out this makes the fear beast even stronger. Instead, we must acknowledge its existence, respect its presence, and work hard to keep our choices and actions aligned with the values we hold dear. Each and every time we stand up to fear with courage and kindness, we hold up a light that says 'fear has no power here'. We serve as a beacon to ourselves and others that the true power lies within us. We create the lives we want and crave by embracing our values and purpose in this world. We show up to our lives with a mightiness that tames the beast. As I frequently say to my clients, this is not work for the faint of heart. Indeed, grappling with fear is the most challenging thing we will do with our lives – and it is also the most rewarding.

I have always found inspiration in the words of thought leaders, spiritual advisors, and poets. Through social media posts I began to add my own narrative to some of these as a way to bring deeper context to fear and to highlight our birthright of choice. This book is a compilation of these posts. I hope, like me, you find inspiration in the pages ahead and find your one unique and powerful voice in order to speak truth to fear.

– PZ

COURAGE

"Without courage we cannot practice any other virtue with consistency. We can't be kind, true, merciful, generous or honest."
– Maya Angelou

Our character is not defined by whether or not we have values (of course we do!), but whether we are able to have alignment between our values and our actions when we are troubled, unsure, confused or scared. Our ability and willingness to embrace courage during difficult times allows for clearer congruency between the values we hold dear and our behaviours. Otherwise, fear will prod us to behave in ways that undermine our truest intentions and sabotage our relationships.

UNIQUENESS

> "It's your road and yours alone. Others can walk it with you, but no one can walk it for you."
> – Rumi

The most important relationship we have is with ourselves. Each of us is literally 'one of a kind' – there will never be another you or me, ever! The journey of knowing who we are, all of it – our amazing brilliance, our unique gifts/talents, our emotional baggage and our dark fears – is totally up to us. This is our power: to understand how we are showing up in our worlds, at home, at work and in our relationships, and to own it all with kindness and a positive self regard. To lovingly embrace our incredible uniqueness takes courage, honesty and compassion – and is the ultimate path to an accountable and meaningful life. How will you befriend yourself today with loving kindness?

COURAGE

"Life shrinks or expands in proportion to one's courage."
– Anaïs Nin

Never let fear choose your future. Face it, own it, embrace it, and proceed willingly into the magnificent edginess of your life.

RESILIENCE

"The only way out is through."
– Robert Frost

In my work with leaders I am often asked how to make challenging situations feel easier. Really what they (and all of us!) want to know is if there is something – a piece of information, some research, a new understanding – that can help ease the discomfort around the uncertainty, stress and fear that often accompany challenging events and people. Here is what I believe: changing the uncomfortable and challenging properties of difficult situations does not generate real learning. It is our willingness to see, accept and lean into the difficulty and then to engage in the meaningful, kind and truthful conversations with others that not only elevate our learning but have the potential to create transformation. Yes, it's messy and uncomfortable, but necessary to get lasting and meaningful results. The truth is it never gets easier but we can get better at choosing the resilient path.

AWARENESS

"Please do not feed the fears."

Avoidance, denial and blame fuel our fears. A meaningful and connected life requires that we know, own, and share our stories. This is what supports understanding, empathy and growth.

TRUTH

"Bold, courageous truth."

Speaking our truth despite our fear is what transforms lives and cultures. This is often painful, messy and uncomfortable but necessary to generate any real and sustainable change.

RESILIENCE

"The pose begins when we want to leave it."
– B.K.S. Iyengar

Yoga, work, relationships, life - in the edginess of our experience is where the wisdom lives. Everything else is just more information. Where is your edge today?

LOVE

"There are a hundred paths through the world that are easier than loving. But who wants easier?"
– Mary Oliver

It is an act of soulful love, this willingness to show up to each other with the deep intention of knowing and being known. It is through surrendering our defensiveness and entering into the gritty and vulnerable discussions that we are able to more fully see, understand, know and love each other. The easier path – led by fear – is to turn away from the edginess through judgment, or anger, or blame, or shame or even hate. Fear's response to deep human connection is always 'No' and 'Don't'. Our choice – though more difficult – must be to say 'Yes' to love and find a way to speak our truths to each other with kindness and a longing to understand.

AWARENESS

"The real voyage of discovery consists not in seeking new landscapes, but in having new eyes."
– Marcel Proust

The biggest learning moments in my life have always happened when I have been willing to understand the stories I have about people and situations and the purpose these stories serve. A powerful question in times of conflict, stress or fear is: what story am I telling myself about this? This allows for a deeper truth to emerge in order to generate a more positive and meaningful outcome. Transformation is always an inside job. What stories are you telling yourself?

FEAR

> "Come to the edge
> We might fall
> Come to the edge
> It's too high
> Come to the edge
> And they came
> and he pushed
> and they flew"
> – Christopher Logue

As long as I can remember this has been a favourite quote of mine. I cite it often in workshops and in my work with leaders. I also use this quote in my own life as a sort of mantra – it serves as a reminder that fear's answer to everything is 'no' and 'don't', and it inspires me to say 'yes' to life thus choosing more bold and courageous action. Complacency can only ever yield more of the same. Let's all ask where in our lives we wish to have more success, more joy, more love, more kindness...and lean into our own edginess by speaking our truths to the fears that hold us back from the richness of life.

CHOICE

"We are our choices."
– J.P Sartre

We are the sum accumulation of our choices. It is not what we think or feel or intend that counts – it is what we repeatedly do that ultimately matters. I have never met anyone – including myself – that didn't want to have a happy and successful life filled with abundance, joy and love. And yet, at times our behaviours contradict this. Life math is simple (although exceedingly difficult at times!): if you want kindness, be kind; if you want connection, reach out; if you want love, be loving; if you want choices, be brave. Otherwise, we will spin our wheels perpetually in fear and rumination which at best will leave us feeling misunderstood and at worst unwanted or unloved. Where in your life can you choose to do what you need?

UNIQUENESS

"If you are always trying to be normal, you will never know how amazing you can be."
– Maya Angelou

Feeling we belong is a very deep human need. In order to be accepted by others, we often try to conform to a set of conditions that will give us membership to a group, a clique, a job, a hobby or vocation. It is so easy to lose our way as we water down who we are in order to fit in with others, and when we don't or can't, it can feel that somehow we are not normal or 'good enough'. The truth is that every one of us is unique and we each have such special gifts to give to each other and the world. The most important place to feel we belong, then, is with ourselves first – to appreciate and value who we are and what we have to bring that is unlike any other offering. How can we truly see and claim our own amazingness? Perhaps then we wouldn't need to 'fit in' at all and we could let our own lights shine more brightly.

AWARENESS

"I must be a mermaid, I have no fear of depths and a great fear of shallow living."
–Anaïs Nin

I have always been a deeply and soulfully curious person and I have been very fortunate to build a life and a career that allows me to take deep dives into the human conditions that motivate behaviours. Our ability to achieve the life we want – both personal and professional – is in direct proportion to our willingness to go past the surface markers through the murky darkness of our fears, and reach into the deep stillness of the truths that ultimately guide our mindsets and decisions. Otherwise, we are perpetually at the mercy of the waves. Deep sea diving anyone?

UNIQUENESS

"If the path before you is perfectly clear you are
probably on someone else's."
– Joseph Campbell

Don't coast on someone else's proven path. Create your own! What makes our unique journey difficult is also what gives our life meaning. I'd rather be a pioneer than a settler. How about you?

INTEGRITY

"Our inner and outer worlds must meet or our lives will crush us."

Our journeys are not all the same. Knowing, owning, relishing and bravely sharing ourselves in all our roles – partner, parent, leader – in every part of our lives. This is how we create a life that flourishes. This is how we successfully and meaningfully attend to the things that are important to us. When we fail to understand or accept our true gifts, we can only present to the world a stunted version of ourselves; one that is incongruent with our true nature and can only ever ultimately generate a sense of diminishment, regret and disappointment. We can all cultivate a deep trust in ourselves and our truths and courageously share this with the world. How will you do this today?

BELIEF

"With each sunrise we start anew."

It never ceases to amaze me that no matter how rainy, snowy, or foggy it is on the ground, when an airplane ascends past the cloud cover there is an endless horizon of blue or starry sky. The same holds true about our fears. They keep us living life smaller than we truly want, or stuck in repeating patterns of frustration or pain. When we are able to rise above these limiting beliefs we can see the endless possibilities that have always been there, just waiting for us to arrive.

CHOICE

"Why live an ordinary life when you can live an extraordinary one?"
– Tony Robbins

Every single moment of every single day we are choosing the quality and meaning of our lives. Each of us has the ongoing opportunity to bring more deliberate passion, love, and kindness with each and every one of these choices. How are you showing up in your own life today?

CALM

"Calm is where our power resides."

Our ability to move through our lives with strength and stability is proportionate to the calm foundation we have cultivated within ourselves. Physically. Mentally. Emotionally. How have you developed your inner reservoir of power? How can you summon it when needed? Calm = the origin of all superpowers.

FEAR

"Let difficulty transform you. And it will. In my experience, we just need help in learning how not to run away."
– Pema Chodrom

How do you get in your own way? Turning to face our fears is the single most important thing we can do for our growth and development. The process of naming, accepting, and then disabling fear's influence is the only pathway that creates sustainable transformation. But fear is tricky; it will masquerade as many things, leading us to believe that our circumstances or other people are the real problem and leaving us to believe we are powerless. And we are not. It is edgy and uncomfortable but necessary work. Ask yourself: what are you afraid of? What would you do if you weren't afraid?

CHOICE

"Everyone must choose one of two pains: the pain of discipline or the pain of regret."
– Jim Rohn

We all know the truth. There are no magic bullets, secret formulas, or short cuts. Success in work or life is the result of assessing what is most important and then following through with the actions that move us closer to that reality. Even if it feels edgy, even if we feel unsure, even if it scares us...we still do it. The powerful quality of discipline is to summon the concerted effort even when it is uncomfortable or difficult and to learn never to negotiate with ourselves to wait until it feels easier. It never will, and all that will be left is regret. What action can you take today that will bring you closer to what really matters to you?

UNIQUENESS

"What you do makes a difference and you have to decide what kind of difference you want to make."
– Jane Goodall

Each of us impacts the world by what we do and what we don't do. How will you make a difference today?

COURAGE

"It's not enough to be nice in life. You've got to have nerve."
– Georgia O'Keeffe

Meaningful living requires a balance of kindness and courage. One without the other is not enough if we want to successfully pursue our purpose, passions, or dreams. How do you generate a satisfying equilibrium between bravery and caring?

UNIQUENESS

"The world is going to judge you no matter what you do – so live your life the way you want."

With kindness and purpose, be who you are. The world needs you!

WORTHINESS

> "No power on earth can destroy the thirst for human dignity."
> – Nelson Mandela

Feeling worthy is a non-negotiable human need. Every one of us needs to feel that we matter. Every one of us needs to feel that we are making a difference. It is not a question of whether or not we are actively seeking to get these needs met (because we are), but rather the awareness, insight and skill we bring to HOW we are getting these needs met that makes the difference. This is the work of leadership: to inspire and influence working conditions and interactions that support the day to day, deliberate, and positive expressions of human dignity. How thirsty are the people in your organization? How thirsty are you?

FEAR

"Avoiding danger is no safer in the long run than outright exposure. The fearful are caught as often as the bold."
– Helen Keller

Fear tricks us into believing that we are safer if we are overly careful and work hard not to rock too many boats. All this creates is a small life... and even bigger fear. What would it mean if you stood your ground with fear and embraced the boldness that resides within you?

COURAGE

"Great courage is not demonstrated by aggression or ambition, which are often expressions of fear or delusion. The courageous heart is the one that is unafraid to open to the world."
– Jack Kornfield

While driving yesterday I came upon an accident that had just happened. A car had hit a deer and the poor thing lay dead in the middle of the road. Traffic was reduced to a crawl as drivers needed to maneuver around the debris of both the carcass and some car bits. As I made my way past the doe I caught her lifeless eye and I was instantly filled with an intense sorrow. Continuing down the road I tried to push this feeling away, first by diminishing the event (it was just a deer), then by translating the event (no human was hurt, thank heavens) and then by finding blame for it (maybe the driver wasn't paying attention). Eventually and finally I just settled into the sadness itself, being open to it, allowing it to fill my heart and all I could feel was compassion for everyone involved – both human and doe – in this awful accident. I thought about how often we brace and harden ourselves against the sorrows and hardships of life instead of just allowing them to soften our hearts, thereby creating suppleness, fortitude, and courage – all of which the world needs more of.

CHOICE

"In the end we regret the chances we didn't take."

Showing up to our own life with kindness, love, and passionate resolve takes courage. What would it mean for you to choose more engagement in the activities and interactions that feed your soul with meaning and purpose? What would it mean to the world? In the words of Lee Ann Womack, "if you get a chance to sit it out or dance...I hope you dance".

CHOICE

"If you plan on being anything less than you are capable of being, you will probably be unhappy all the days of your life."
– Abraham Maslow

Our inner purpose and longings are always calling. Saying yes to the potential of who we are takes courage and leads to the ultimate success of life: a profound sense of well being. How will you say yes today?

CHOICE

"In any moment of decision the best thing you can do is the right thing. The next best thing you can do is the wrong thing. The worst thing you can do is nothing."
– Theodore Roosevelt

Action creates growth and/or learning. Inaction – waiting or hoping or analysis – generates the status quo/repeated patterns/more of the same. What do you choose today?

CHOICE

"You will be exactly as happy as you decide to be."

Happiness is a choice. That is all.

UNIQUENESS

"Walk with the dreamers, the believers, the courageous, the cheerful, the planners, the doers, the successful people with their heads in the clouds and their feet on the ground. Let their spirit ignite a fire within you to leave this world better than when you found it."
– Wilfred A. Peterson

The world needs us all to live our fiery purpose. The one that is ours and ours alone to make the difference that only we can make. Each of us truly matters more than we can ever know.

JOY

"There are only two ways to live your life. One is as though nothing is a miracle. The other is as though everything is a miracle."
– Albert Einstein

Life is amazing, joyful, painful, happy, lonely, exciting, sad, fulfilling, confusing, loving, fearful, thrilling, and simply glorious. And we get to experience all of it. If that is not a miracle, what is?

FEAR

"What if I fall? Oh, but my darling, what if you fly?"
– Erin Hanson

When we allow fear to predict the outcome before we begin, we never find out the strength of our wings.

CHOICE

"Nothing outside you can ever give you what you're looking for."
– Byron Katie

The ultimate currency of life is a good and positive sense of well being. Nothing external, no matter how comforting or seductive, can ever sustainably provide us with this. It is always an inside job and our experience of joy, peace and love is always up to us. How are you choosing your well being today?

CHOICE

"Until you make the unconcious concious, it will direct your life, and you will call it fate."
– Carl Jung

A meaningful life never just happens. It takes concerted effort and awareness of self – even the dark and shadowy parts – to bring deliberate consciousness to our world. Knowing and aligning our inner values with our outer circumstances and relationships is how we can courageously craft the truest and strongest sense of wellbeing and meaning. It's also how we inspire and support others to do the same. Choice, then, is more powerful than fate. What will you choose today?

CHOICE

"Everything in your life is a reflection of a choice you have made. If you want a different result, make a different choice."

Choice is our human birthright. Every behaviour, every thought, and every feeling is ours alone to choose, regardless of external influences and circumstances. Every moment I have ever had of stuckness, hopelessness, and suffering is from embracing the fear instead of the freedom of this reality. And every 'aha', transformative, and healing moment I have had is because I embraced the freedom instead of the fear.

COURAGE

"Integrity is choosing courage over comfort; choosing what is right over what is fun, fast or easy; and choosing to practice our values rather than simply professing them."
– Brené Brown

This Brené Brown quote is such a gem in our easy-fix, multi-tasking, comfort focused, instant gratification culture. Right action seldom, if ever, feels like the easier choice. In fact, it most often feels like the toughest as we leave our surefooted comfort zone and step into the far more edgier terrain of emotions, fears, and feeling unsure. And yet, time and time again the most meaningful, high quality, and sustainable decisions, interactions, and solutions are created because we had the courage to step over the cutting edge into the messy discomfort of the unknown.

CHOICE

"The breeze at dawn has secrets to tell you
Don't go back to sleep
You must ask for what you really want
Don't go back to sleep
People are going back and forth across the door sill
Where the two worlds touch
The door is round and open
Don't go back to sleep"
– Rumi

Staying awake to our truth is the challenge of life. Fear will lull us back to sleep – to living numbed down, dumbed down, half conscious lives, where the promise of something different and truer always lives in tomorrow. Yet the door is always open, and the choice is always ours. Which side of the threshold are you living in today?

JOY

"Always believe that something wonderful is about to happen."

One of the capacities for a meaningful and successful life is unbridled optimism. Seeing the good in what has been, what is, and what is yet to come is a mindset that combines both a grateful heart and a hopeful spirit. How will you embrace wonder today?

CHOICE

"May your choices reflect your hopes, not your fears."
– Nelson Mandela

Every decision we make is either about moving toward or away from something. The hopeful energy of moving toward is life affirming, transformative, and generates self-efficacy. The fearful energy of moving away drains our spirit, creates resentment, and disempowers us. Hope creates power and fear creates pain. Let us all choose wisely.

COURAGE

> "There is a difference between knowing the path and walking the path."
> – Morpheus, *The Matrix*

The gap between knowing and doing inhibits progress and stymies growth. Amazing insight, sophisticated understanding, and brilliant wisdom are nice, but only action produces success and only bold, courageous action generates transformation. What are you allowing to get in the way between what you know and what you do?

FEAR

"If it's both terrifying and amazing then you should definitely pursue it."
– Erada Svetlana

Our most meaningful accomplishments always feel risky. Or maybe meaning is the self generated result because we choose to experience the edge and learn. Either way, follow your fiery purpose – it is so worth it!

RESILIENCE

"Everything will be okay in the end. If it's not okay,
it's not the end."
– John Lennon

It's OK for things not to be OK.

We may at times feel hopeful and at other times discouraged.

We may feel energized by the possibilities that await and then disheartened with the realization that things will never be quite the same.

This messy ride of life can feel like a rollercoaster. Knowing we are always co-creating a new way together, all while we grieve the loss of what was and fear what will be.

And it is necessary – all of it. This is the place where the real work of growth and transformation begins. And it is important we embrace the glorious learnings contained in both the highs and the lows.

MEANING

"Our anxiety does not come from thinking about the
future but in wanting to control it."
– Khalil Gibran

Living can create such uncertainty about the future. What will our lives look like next week, next month, next season, next year? It can, at times, be hard to imagine as we move into the unknown. Making plans and generating strategies can feel worrisome and risky as there is no way to know if they will yield success. And yet, we also know that doing nothing and just waiting to see what the future has in store for us will not serve our best interests.

The ultimate challenge in life is to continue to show up and do our best despite the uncertainty.

To continue to plan for the future all while staying unattached to a specific outcome. This necessitates having steadfast values, unwavering confidence in ourself and unyielding courage. This is how we create a meaningful reality:

Doing our best even while we know we do not have control over what will happen.

How are you navigating into your unknown future?

COURAGE

"Conflictmorphosis"

Conflictmorphosis (noun)

1) A notable difference in our habits around uncomfortable experiences and relationships.

2) A process by which our beliefs about a person or situation (especially ones we find difficult) transform into something new.

3) Something different is created because of uncertainty, adversity or conflict.

FEAR

"You are more powerful than what you fear."

Fear is only as powerful as we allow it to be. It has no strength of its own, only what we give it. Fear is a trickster, a grand illusionist who will never stop trying to convince us that it is more important than our hopes, dreams, and goals. The decision is always ours – do we acquiesce to fear, or do we claim our birthright of choice? It is the ultimate act of self care and respect to nourish our soul by owning our authority to act in accordance to our deepest values and purpose.

INTEGRITY

"Integrity is the greatest gift we can give to ourself."

When our behaviour aligns with our internal values, we are powerful beyond measure. Doing what we know to be right is a more difficult path, but it is also the only way to develop confidence in our self-efficacy. Following the lure of pleasure, comfort, or acceptance may feel easier, but in the end we sacrifice our authority in the world as we are always at the whim of external circumstance and other people. With courage and discipline, let us all find more ways to know and own our truest values and 'walk our talk'. We are worth it and the world is in need of our authentic presence.

INTEGRITY

"The energy of the mind is the essence of life."
– Aristotle

Our internal energy is what determines the success and meaning in our lives. We have to first clearly know our values before we can act on them. We must have a positive and meaningful relationship with ourselves first before we can have one with others. We must first believe in our ability to have a positive impact before we can truly advance our purpose in the world. The quality and nature of all external energy will always align with our true internal energy. This is law – no matter how sophisticated, clever, and witty we present ourselves as to the world, what we really believe about ourselves will always define the quality of our lives. So let's all stop trying to 'fake it till you make it' – a false positive is actually a negative. And false positive energy is non-sustainable energy because there is no real source to nourish and renew it. Let's move past the shallowness of tricks and tips, beyond the superficial appearances, and away from any notion that there are ever any shortcuts. All we are doing is painting a wet board. It looks all shiny, bright, and new for a day, maybe two, but inevitably, predictably, and very quickly the paint will flake and peel away because there is nothing to adhere to. Instead, let's dig much deeper into who we are, peeling away the layers of fear and confusion that block our inner power, by claiming the true authority of who we are and deliberating discharging that into our lives and into the world. This positive and powerful energy is always there for every single one of us to affirm and proclaim. This is also law.

RESILIENCE

"You cannot find peace by avoiding life."

I have often thought that having inner peace is akin to the experience after a good workout. The pure and clear bliss of showing up and doing my best through the push and the pull. Digging into and moving through the discomfort (at times feeling it is impossible) and exuberantly relishing in the sweat, the movement, and the rush. Feeling utterly spent and yet energized for more – knowing I have given it my all and that I will again. This is how I get to experience peace: embracing all of what life has to offer, and showing up to the joy and the challenge. Knowing if I avoid owning the negative and turn away from the fear I will deny myself the positive and miss out on the magic of the unbridled joy of life. The experience of inner peace is not a passive one; it is a very activated state of feeling thoroughly exhausted, completely engaged, and fully alive. What is your experience with inner peace?

TRUTH

"The conversation is the relationship."
– Susan Scott

The quality of our relationships is determined by the nature of the conversations we are having. In the simplest terms – meaningful relationships require ongoing meaningful dialog involving the mutual sharing of inner needs, feelings, and fears.

To know and be known is a primal human element need that is essential to our well being. As such, it is important that we are able to share more about how we are really feeling – our hopes, fears, joys, and sorrows – for this is what binds us to each other and brings meaning to our life.

Otherwise, the best we can hope for is friendly surface talk around external and safe topics (eg. weather, casual activities, ailments, other people, etc.) which not only leaves little or no opportunity to experience a deeper connection with others, but often leaves us feeling disconnected and alone in our experiences of both joy and pain.

Who are the important people in your life? What would happen if you shared 5% more than you normally did about your inner emotional reality? What would happen if, through kindness, caring, and curiosity, we ask others to share more of their inner world?

It has been said that we are born alone and we will die alone. In between these two events we get to share this exquisite and miraculous journey of life with others; why not make it the most meaningful experience possible through rich and soulful sharing?

UNIQUENESS

"I am here."

Who am I? What are my true needs and desires? What is the best way for me to serve?

Others may help us or hinder us, but the answers cannot be found externally – they can only be known from within, at the centre of our being. We must belong to ourselves first by embracing and expressing our fiery heart's purpose.

Only then will we feel at home in the world.

FEAR

"On the other side of fear lies freedom."

Every time we are faced with adversity we have a choice.

We can succumb to the lure of fear calling us downward into the destructive energy of avoidance, anger and cynicism. Generating hopelessness, defeat and ultimately greater fear.

Or, we can embrace the creative energy of curiosity, caring and openness. Initiating learning, growth and transformation.

This is freedom. Seeing our choice, even as the darkness encroaches on us. With deliberation and focused effort, choosing the path that leads to an optimistic future.

Fear and freedom always exist simultaneous, fed by the same energy of stress, tension, uncertainty and conflict. In all of our challenges, big and small, we choose which side we invest in.

What would it mean to you and your challenges to feel more freedom and less fear?

FEAR

> "Darkness has a hunger that's insatiable and lightness has a call that's hard to hear."
> – Indigo Girls

The only way to get to the light is to go through the darkness that wants to devour us. This is no small feat! All of our fears, insecurities, past baggage, failures, traumas, and anxieties will be whispering in our ear. Prodding or cajoling us back and insisting that we will never make it, so why bother trying at all? Convincing us we are not strong enough and we don't deserve it anyway. The darkness will have us stop in our tracks, repeating the same old limiting patterns of self belief. And yet, there is always another choice available to us if we stay awake and look to the horizon.

Time and time and time again we must re-orient ourselves to the small yet mighty distant beacon, the siren call of our soul. Ignoring darkness' greed, we can move further into our own, wondrous, amazing, and powerful lightness of being.

WORTHINESS

> "The greatest gift we have to offer is knowing our worth."

In several conversations this week with clients and friends, I noticed a common theme. People undermining their value, minimizing their role, and not fully sharing their voice. Yet, in every case, they had so much more to offer and say, and were holding themselves back. Each person was robbing the world of the unique gift only they can offer because of either not knowing or not embracing their distinct perspective and extraordinary abilities, and ultimately not seeing their own true worth. The greatest gift we can ever give is the one we give to ourselves: of knowing our worth. What would it mean to you to own your worth? What would it mean to the world?

COURAGE

"Conflict seldom survives heartfelt intention and sincere curiosity."

Every single time we avoid our conflicts, they grow stronger and we become less powerful.

Every single time we deny our conflicts, we withhold from ourselves the opportunity to grow and to increase our self efficacy.

Becoming a better human, parent, friend, partner, team member, or leader is difficult work. It takes courage to embrace the frustration, confusion, pain, anger, fear, hopelessness, and vulnerability that comes hand in hand with the conflicts we experience.

And yet, it is the only way in which we can truly own our power in this world. And it is the only way to solve our problems and transform our conflicts.

What would happen if you approached your biggest conflicts with the fierce and focused energy of open heartedness and sincere questioning? What will happen if you don't?

AWARENESS

> "Courage to begin
> Heart to continue
> Grit to finish."

The energy which inspires us to initiate a new course or begin a new goal is not the same energy that sustains us in the messy middle or propels us through the last mile over a finish line. Success in anything requires we tap into our diverse inner strengths at different points along the journey. Otherwise, we risk false starts, or feeling underwhelmed with our results. Or worse yet, perpetually stuck in a muddle, feeling there is no way forward and no way back. Where are you on the path?

FEAR

"Fear is a liar."

If you find yourself fearing you are not enough, feeling you are not worthy or significant or smart or beautiful or capable enough, either because you are telling yourself this or someone else is (either by what they say or what they won't say to you), know this: fear is a liar. You are more than enough, so dig deep, beautiful souls, and move out of the darkness and embrace your unique power and fiery truth.

INTEGRITY

"Unintentional doesn't equal not responsible."

What is beneath intention?

How are we able to connect the dots between our actions or inactions and the impacts we are actually having? So often we will say "this wasn't what I meant" or "it wasn't my intention" as a way to explain ourselves. And then, because we truly didn't mean any harm, it is easy to disown our contribution into what does exist.

My work in organizations takes me into the dreadful stress of conflict and adversity. To help people directly address the conditions which are negative, frustrating, and painful and create something that is more positive, rewarding, and meaningful for everyone. But this can only happen when each of us can see and own our role in what currently exists. Otherwise we will hold others accountable and not ourselves. And nothing will change.

What is beneath intention? Accountability. Knowing we have played a part even when we are unsure or confused about what that means. Having the courage, conviction and compassion to ask the questions of ourselves and to engage in the important conversations with others. This is where leadership is no longer a role but an immutable responsibility to ourselves and others.

CHOICE

"Your attention please: no one is coming to save you. This life of yours is 100% your responsibility."

An immutable law of life: personal responsibility is absolute. This means it is up to each of us to design our own life in a way that feels meaningful, purposeful, and useful. And we can – we are that powerful! So no more need to wait for anything or to blame anyone, because a successful and happy life is of our own choosing. Always has been and always will be. Isn't this the best news ever?

GRATITUDE

"Gratitude changes everything."

When I am bitching I can't be thankful, and when I am thankful I can't be bitching. It is not joy that makes us grateful; it is gratitude that makes us joyful.

TRUTH

"You are not alone."

Everyone struggles at times. We all have felt pain, confusion, frustration, desperation, and loneliness. The true hero is the one who speaks out about these things, normalizes them, and reaches out to others to let them know they are never alone. Suffering can only be reduced through our connection with others. Who will you connect with today?

UNIQUENESS

"The world will ask you who you are, and if you
don't know, the world will tell you."
– Carl Jung

You are the boss of you. No one else. You decide your values and your purpose in this world. Sing it from the mountain top and proclaim it for all to hear.

CHOICE

"Energy cannot be created or destroyed, it can only be changed from one form to another."
– Albert Einstein

The choice that exists within all difficult moments, large and small, is how we use the energy of adversity to either make our way back to some familiar way or use it to learn and grow.

Within adversity lies the potential for a future that is more meaningful and fulfilling for all. But with every storm is risk of loss and if we don't pay attention, fear will lead our way. Our need for momentary comfort and familiarity will have us disconnect and retreat and the opportunity for transformation will be lost until the next storm.

Only then, it will be more difficult and painful as our beliefs and habits have further solidified.

This is our challenge with all adversity. How to utilize the energetic tension for positive change.

Let's be honest, if we won't approach our ordinary, daily problems and conflicts with this perspective, how will we ever be successful with the unprecedented and historic ones?

TRUTH

"Every decision you make arises from who you believe you are and reflects the value you place on yourself."

Don't settle for anything less than the truth of who you are – not even from yourself. Are we not our own worst enemy when it comes to believing in our worthiness and power? Is this not an unending source of frustration and pain for ourselves and others? Living small and dimming our light robs the world of your unique gifts. And the world needs everyone to stand tall and proud in their unique brilliance. Believe in yourself – you are so worth it!

CHOICE

"Never let fear decide your future."

Our outer journey must begin inside. First knowing our worth. Then owning our purpose and values so we can show up in the world on our own terms. Choosing courage over fear again and again and again.

AWARENESS

"You get what you tolerate."
– Henry Cloud

Tolerate: VERB ['tälə,rāt] to allow the existence, occurrence, or practice of something that one does not necessarily like or agree with without interference (Oxford Dictionary); to endure difficulty and pain without hinderance (Merriam-Webster). What are you putting up with in your life that no longer serves you?

CALM

"It is inner stillness that will save and transform the world."
– Eckhart Tolle

Beneath our thoughts, feelings, and fiery purpose lies our true power: the calm, benevolent, and certain presence of our connection with the universe.

RESILIENCE

"If you're invested into security and certainty, you are on the wrong planet."
– Pema Chödrön

Playing small and being careful never safeguards us from the risk of living. So embrace your inner power, dig into your fiery purpose, and boldly walk your own path through this one short life.

AWARENESS

"There is no one alive that hasn't wanted to go back to sleep."
– Elizabeth Lesser

The ultimate act of self care is staying awake to your life. Don't heed the inevitable siren call of the unconsciousness. It will lure you into vague acquiescence and diminish your astonishing presence in the world. The world needs you to awaken to your unique and brilliant power.

JOY

"Be a seeker of everyday magic."

I felt such beauty and awe experiencing the full moon before today's dawn. Such a loving reminder that magic, wonder, and joy are always here – around us and within us. All we have to do is just look.

UNIQUENESS

"As far as we can discern, the sole purpose of human existence is to kindle a light in the darkness of mere being."
– Carl Jung

We are all bound together in this human-ness. Struggling to find our way through the darkness and uncertainty, longing to know we matter to others, and hoping we make a difference in the world. How are you letting your light shine? How are you honouring and appreciating the light in others?

CHOICE

"Life is too short to be unhappy at work."

If you work full time, you will spend upwards to 100,000 hours at work in your lifetime. Removing childhood and senior years, this means spending a third of your waking life at work.

Or more.

The statistics on the quality of our work lives are grim. Research shows that 75% of workers report, at best, a lack lustre experience and, at worst, one that is defined by mind numbing stress and dread.

Isn't it time we rethink the sheer importance to our lives that the quality of our work experience has?

UNIQUENESS

"If my aim is to prove I am 'enough', the project will go on to infinity – because the battle was already lost the day I conceded the issue was debatable."
– Nathaniel Branden

Of course you are enough. You always have been and always will be. The real challenge lies in seeing and believing this truth. It is always an inside job.

INTEGRITY

"You are 100% responsible for the energy you bring into a room."

Our presence and influence is experienced by others not just by what we say and do, but also in what we think and how we feel. Our internal world – our beliefs, judgements, and intentions – can never be truly hidden, no matter how skilled we are at presenting ourselves to the external world. Authentic leadership is about aligning our internal and external energies in a way that brings congruency to what we say and what our true beliefs are. This is the tough work for all of us: building trust, and inspiring others by initiating the truthful and important conversations.

COURAGE

"All progress takes place outside of the comfort zone."

No exceptions: growth requires a willingness and ability to deliberately choose to be uncomfortable.

RESILIENCE

"It's not about making it easier..."

What are you waiting for? All of us have experienced life's difficulties. From minor annoyances to formidable challenges, we have all been there. And it can be so hard, sometimes excruciatingly difficult, painful, even debilitating, as we wonder how we will cope with the path ahead. During these moments it is tempting to want to find a way to make the road easier, less bumpy, straighter, with at least some small guarantee that our efforts will be successful in the way we hope. And yet, as we all have experienced and witnessed over and over again – if we have been paying attention – the most meaningful and fulfilling achievements and experiences in our lives are not because the way forward was easy, but because it was difficult and uncertain. It is only by accepting and embracing the difficulties and choosing to purposefully walk forward into the dark unknown that we get better at successfully navigating our formidable challenges. If we wait for things to get easier, we will always miss out on the best that life has to offer us.

COURAGE

"Be brave enough to start a conversation that matters."

One of the non-negotiable abilities of great leadership is the willingness to initiate the conversations that matter. Yet all too often, the fear of engaging in the uncomfortable and edgy dialogs that are necessary to solve tough problems will generate avoidance and/or denial, and we wait, hoping for things to feel easier or clearer. And the issues persist, almost always getting worse. Being able to address problems and conflicts in timely, direct, and caring ways is not intuitive nor natural for most of us. It is a mindset and skillset that must be learned and reinforced again and again. And that is what great leaders do.

How do you navigate the edgy yet necessary conversations?

MEANING

"If there is meaning in life at all, then there must be meaning in suffering."
– Victor Frankl

With great stress and change comes extraordinary opportunity for growth. Powerful questions we can ask during such times are: "How will I change?" and "How will I allow the difficulty of these challenging circumstances to transform me for the better?" I do not believe it is enough to simply endure and suffer through our difficult days, nor to sit by and watch others do the same. Instead, it is incumbent on us to find meaning within our challenges and to ask what can we learn because of this hardship. We never willingly choose the events that create our greatest suffering, ever. We can, however, choose to use them for our greatest learning.

FEAR

"Fear is not in the habit of speaking the truth."
– Tacitus

Fear. Ancient, powerful, and convincing.

Fear manifests in many different ways, driving both our mindset and actions.

At times, fear is proudly on display for all to see and name. At other times, fear is opaque and controls us from an inner obscured place of darkness masquerading under another guise. Fear always pretends to be necessary and is genius at using our own logic against us.

The path to problem solving, creativity, and transformation is in our ability to see fear in all its forms; respecting its presence, but never allowing it to influence our decision making. Can you recognize the many guises of fear?

TRUTH

"Silence always creates a bigger problem than sharing a relevant truth."

As difficult as some conversations are, and as risky as some messages feel, it is always better to have the discussions that focus in on the real, important, and relevant issues. Not only does avoiding or delaying these necessary conversations make matters even worse, it erodes our credibility and diminishes trust. How can you push through the discomfort and find a way to share your truths?

CHOICE

"The quality of our lives depends not on whether or not we have conflicts, but on how we respond to them."
– Thomas Crum

The most common ways to participate in conflict are avoidance and denial with the occasional (and destructive) escalation. This adds up to demoralizing stress, polarized relationships, and disappointing outcomes. There are skillsets everyone can learn to manage conflict in positive ways, and approaches that lead to more fulfillment, enjoyment, and productivity. Isn't it time to commit to a higher quality work and life experience?

RESILIENCE

"Most of us have two lives: the life we live, and the unlived life within us. Between the two stands resistance."
– Steven Pressfield

Resistance is the dream crusher and the fear feeder all at the same time. It is the endless messages and stories we tell ourselves over and over again about why we can't or why we won't follow our heart's purpose or desire. It is every excuse we create about why not and why not right now. It's every limitation we allow to extinguish our internal fiery purpose. Resistance is the hard edge that keeps us living a divided life. With every moment we have the choice to either strengthen the wall of resistance that keeps us in unfulfilling, painful patterns, or to lift the veil of fear and step more fully into our unique, soulful purpose. We are far more powerful than resistance, but only if we choose to be.

MEANING

"Fulfillment is lived from the inside out."

Difficulty and uncertainty create conditions that highlight our power of choice.

Through the tension of adversity our character is challenged and more deliberate effort is required to act in accordance with our values.

It is through struggle we become stronger but only if we see hardship as a catalyst to growth.

Otherwise, we succumb to being only a victim to external circumstances and we forfeit our inner authority in the world.

Harnessing the power of adversity is an essential skillset for a fulfilling life.

RESILIENCE

"Adversity is the mother of progress."
– Mahatma Gandhi

So often our approach to difficulty and uncertainty is to avoid or deny the discomfort and pain it creates. Our energies go toward escaping the discomfort, enduring the stress and waiting/hoping for the adversity to pass. By doing so, we not only forfeit our own learning and growth, we lose the invaluable opportunity for progress to occur within our cultures.

We then go into another day with the same conditions and the same old problems with the same inner longing for something different and something more. And we experience less effectiveness and less fulfillment.

Building significant and sustainable change requires the capacity of conflict tenacity. This is having the mindsets and skillsets able to sustain deliberate awareness and positive effort outside of our comfort zones. It requires initiating and engaging in the difficult – a.k.a. learning – conversations with others.

There is no shortcut. The process is difficult and often messy.

And through it we are rewarded with meaningful growth.

MEANING

"Our ultimate goal – in everything we do – is to experience fulfillment."

Fulfillment. Such a humble word representing something so powerful. Fulfillment is about achievement. Defining our goals, working hard, and getting results. It is the creation of something in the world that exists because we have applied our brilliance.

Fulfillment is also about feeling joy, contentment and gratification. This is our inner experience of satisfaction and pride in ourself for the manner in which we achieved what we did. To feel fulfilled is to act in accordance with our values – and this always involves how we are in relationship with others.

The experience of fulfillment then requires insight, courage, and connection. When one is missing, fulfillment is lacking.

I had a dear mentor who would frequently ask me, "which is more important: the going or the getting"? Of course this is a trick question (as all great questions are). We need both to feel the true success we all long for – making our mark with our work in the world AND knowing we honoured ourself and others in the process.

WORK WITH US

Patricia Zeggelaar is a facilitator, speaker and coach specializing in conflict transformation.

Her work in the world is to help humanize the workplace by supporting and inspiring leaders to effectively and meaningfully manage conflict, stress and negativity.

If you would like support with challenging and stressful situations in your workplace please contact:
>Patricia Zeggelaar
>(902) 476-1642
>info@patriciaz.ca

ABOUT THE AUTHOR

Patricia is on a mission to redefine our relationship with adversity, conflict, and uncertainty. She is passionate about helping people approach difficult situations and relationships in deliberate, respectful, and confident ways generating sustainable problem solving and remarkable growth.

She offers state-of-the-art learning experiences that teach the core competencies of conflict tenacity – that is the skillsets, mindsets, and heartsets that support positive outcomes and satisfying relationship experiences. Whether she is teaching online, implementing workplace diagnostics, or leading immersive retreats, her goal is to help people develop the insight, courage, and endurance to face their fears in order to lead more fulfilling lives.

Patricia is a gritty lifelong learner, a curator of safe space, and a pragmatic problem solver. She has certifications in Organizational Diagnostics, Positive Psychology, Human Element Coaching for Performance, Overcoming Anxiety, Myers Briggs Type Indicator, Herrmann Brain Dominance Indicator, and Trauma Informed Yoga Therapy.

Over the last 25 years, she has boosted the efforts of thousands of leaders and team members to address workplace conflict in effective, meaningful and sustainable ways.

www.ingramcontent.com/pod-product-compliance
Lightning Source LLC
Chambersburg PA
CBHW071422210526
45465CB00001B/496